HOW TO WRITE A NOVEL

STEP-BY-STEP

Essential Romance Novel, Mystery Novel and Fantasy Novel Writing Tricks Any Writer Can Learn

Sandy Marsh

reparation, damages, or monetary loss due to the information herein, either directly or indirectly.

Respective authors own all copyrights not held by the publisher.

The information herein is offered for informational purposes solely, and is universal as so. The presentation of the information is without contract or any type of guarantee assurance.

The trademarks that are used are without any consent, and the publication of the trademark is without permission or backing by the trademark owner. All trademarks and brands within this book are for clarifying purposes only and are the owned by the owners themselves, not affiliated with this document.

Table of Contents

Introduction

Thank you and congratulations on purchasing *"How to Write a Novel: Step-by-Step | Essential Romance Novel, Mystery Novel and Fantasy Novel Writing Tricks Any Writer Can Learn"*. As well, congratulations on deciding that you want to write a fiction novel!

The tips and tricks you will learn in this book will help walk you through the step-by-step process of writing your very own novel, while also making it extremely easy to stay committed! You will learn everything you need to know about simplifying the process and making it one that you can easily stick to so that you can create the fiction novel of your dreams, literally!

Each chapter in this book is dedicated to one part of the novel writing experience. You will begin by learning all about outlines and work your way through each step right down to finding the perfect reader to test out your new novel. By the time you're done reading this you will be completely finished writing your very own fiction novel.

This book was designed to help make the process easier while also making it an enjoyable experience. Understand that this is not necessarily a "conventional" how-to book as it will seek to both educate and inform while also making the process fun and exciting. Writing a book should never be boring or difficult - if it is, you are going about it all wrong! With the steps in this book, you will learn to bring back the passion in your writing and create the best fiction novel possible, whether this is your first time trying or you've done this before and you just need a boost to get through this particular book!

Please be sure to take your time and have fun with this book as the writing process truly is an experience to be enjoyed. Allow each section to provide you with tips and tricks to help lighten up the experience so that you can increase the entertainment you derive from the writing process so that you are left not only with an incredible novel but also with an experience worth remembering. This book can be used as many times as you require, so be sure to keep it handy for any fiction novels you may set out to write! And lastly, please enjoy!

Chapter 1: The Outline

As you may be aware, having an outline to a book is important. This provides you with an idea of where the story is going and what your "goals" for the book are. Many authors prefer to start with a strong outline that will give them direction and help them stay on track when they are working through the writing process. Having a strong outline that identifies major plot points means that you can continually work your story towards each new plot point in chronological order so that you ultimately end up at your "goal" outcome based on what you had included in your outline.

For many writers, an outline is an absolute must-have. They prefer to have an outline that will help guide them because this keeps them focused and working along a credible storyline that is intended to keep readers engaged. By having this the writer knows how to stay on point and how to structure different parts of the story to keep everything working towards the same goal. For others, having an outline feels too boxy and they feel as though their creative expression is being suffocated by the existence of the outline. If this is you, then you may want to consider scratching the outline altogether. Below we will explore different tips and ideas for each unique individual and how you can create an incredible story regardless of whether or not you choose to use an outline.

If You Love to Guide Your Focus…

If you love to have your focus guided towards a particular goal, such as the one at the end of your outline, then having an outline is a good idea for you. This will help encourage you to stay on track with your writing process and keep each unique element of the story focused towards the outcome. Having the outline helps you avoid yourself from putting unnecessary information in the plot line or otherwise over-explaining things that may not be relevant to the overall story itself.

Outlines are a great tool to help keep writers focused and guided throughout the process. Creating an outline is fairly simple, you think of where you want the characters to "start" and "end" in the story. Then, you decide what major plot points are going to get them from the start to the end. For example, you might have two characters in a romance novel that are going to start as best friends and end as lovers. Along the way, you might choose to include plot points such as them taking on a big project together and it brings them closer, but the competitiveness between them drives them apart. As they work through the competitiveness they discover that their relationship grows even stronger and when they complete the project they are feeling closer than ever before. Later they make excuses to hang out even more, and eventually, they end up falling in love. As you can see from this example, the outline included the main characters, the starting and ending points of the story, and major events that lead the two characters to the "finish line".

Once you have created your basic outline, you want to include even more information in it. This would include settings where each scene takes place, the emotions behind each experience, and anything else that would contribute to you setting the mental image for the scene itself. By identifying as many descriptive factors about each major plot point as possible you make it easier for you to know exactly where you are working towards in each part of the story. Of course, you can always choose to alter these if the writing process brings you towards a different idea or plot point, but having them identified and a rough outline created can help you stay on track and remain focused on what you want to take place within' the story.

If you are someone who tends to need tools such as outlines to help you stay focused and guide you through the process it is a good idea that you complete one before you start writing any part of your novel. Having the outline written and in front of you can help you identify what you like about the story and any issues that you may notice before you actually begin writing. This can help you finalize what your conflict will be an anchor in any specific details that you want to include in your writing so that you go into your novel with a clear plan and an idea of how you are going to achieve what you have set out to accomplish.

If You Love Creative Freedom...

If you are the type of writer who prefers to work alongside creative freedom and who feels suffocated by the idea of having a specific plan to work with there are a few things that you can do in order to exercise your creative freedom while still creating an incredible novel. Just because you don't want to have a specific plan doesn't mean that you cannot create some form of a plan that will help you stay focused and work towards some form of goal throughout your novel.

It is important to understand that even if you prefer having creative freedom, you still need to have some form of outline in place to help you organize your plot and stay focused towards a particular goal. This will help ensure that your book flows in such a way that people will read it and easily work towards the goal with you, rather than attempting to understand why there are so many different pieces of information floating around that seem irrelevant to the book itself.

The first idea you could use is to create a vague outline for your book. This would require you to create an ideal starting point and ending point for your novel, and then fill out the inside of the outline with a few different major plot points that will help guide you from point a to point b. Unlike a complete outline, you will only include enough information to give you a general idea of what you want to include in your book. Then, you can come up with the rest as you are in the process of writing your novel. This can help you with allowing you to have creative expression while also staying focused on the purpose of your novel and working towards it while successfully bringing your reader along with you. Ultimately, it prevents the buildup of irrelevant information or you involving anything that is not necessary to the novel itself.

It will, however, allow you to pick out the details and other smaller factors as you go so that you can allow the story to flow through you naturally, rather than feeling pressured to use extremely specific points in varying areas of your story, potentially taking away from the natural flow that you have created through your creative expression.

Another method you can use is called a hindsight outline. The only two things you need to identify in the beginning of creating this outline is the starting and ending points. You should always have some form of end goal when it comes to writing a novel so that you are clear on what you are writing towards and what you need to be building up to throughout the novel. However, with a hindsight outline, you do not need to include any information beyond these two points. All you have to do is ensure that you are working towards the end goal. As you write major plot points into your story, you can then write them into your outline. This may seem irrelevant, but you will soon understand that writing them down allows you to see where you have come from and where you want to go. It ensures that each part of the plot works together towards the goal and that it makes sense towards the overall story. Doing this prevents you from forgetting about plot points, including ones that may contradict previous ones, and get a general idea of the flow of your story in retrospect, rather than in advance.

Questions to Ask Yourself

The following questions are questions you should ask yourself when you are developing your outline. This will ensure that you have a strong plan for your outline and that no details are missed out on.

1. Where is my protagonist starting?

2. Where are they at in their life in the beginning of the story?

3. Where is my protagonist ending?

4. Where are they at in their life at the end of the story?

5. What major plot points are getting me to (or have gotten me to) the goal?

6. Do these plot points make sense together?

7. Is there anywhere that this outline is weak?

8. What else could I add to my outline to make a rich
    reading experience?

How you choose to create the outline for your story is
unique to you and your writing preferences. Know that you are
not required to create a detailed or complete outline before you
begin writing your novel. However, having an outline is
extremely important as it helps you keep major plot points in
chronological order and to ensure that they flow well together.
Still, if you prefer to write it out in detail ahead of time, or if you
prefer to merely identify your goal and create your outline in
hindsight, that is entirely up to you. You should never let creating
an outline and identifying specific details of your story hold you
back from writing the story in the first place. Knowing that there
are options for you to help you stay focused or open up your
creative freedom as much as you need to can help ensure that you
are not intimidated by the very first step of writing your book. It
also helps you feel confident knowing that you can stay focused
and still create an incredible book, whether you do it the
conventional way or not.

Chapter 2: Your Setting

Developing the setting for your story provides you with the opportunity to have an incredible amount of creative expression. This part of the book is also one of the first times that you will begin to get very descriptive about what is going to happen within' your book. Even if you have a complete outline that is quite detailed, this will be more defined than that.

Your setting is ultimately when and where your story happens. This is something that you need to identify beforehand so that you can keep this information flowing throughout the entire story. For example, you wouldn't want to begin writing a story that was set in the 1800s and then use slang or information that was only relevant to the 2000s or later. Identifying your setting and being very specific and clear on it ensures that your entire book is written with relevance to that setting. The following information will help you identify important tips and tricks that you should pay attention to when it comes to developing your setting for your novel.

If You Only Have One Location

If you are writing a book where the story will never venture away from your primary overall location, then you want to make sure that you are very clear and specific on this location. This is where your entire book is going to be written, so you want to be very descriptive of and clear on this location by knowing exactly what is relevant to it and what is true about it.

You should identify where this location is, what sets it apart from other locations, and why you are using this location. You also want to discover what the local culture is like (specific to your time frame) and any other identifying factors that you may learn about this place. The best way to do it is to research this place as though you were going to be a tourist. Make sure that you do it specific to the time frame, which you will learn more about in a moment. For the location-specific part, however, you want to identify what types of buildings exist in this place, what they were made of, what the roads looked like, what types of wildlife and plant life exists in the area, and anything else that will help you create a graphic image in someone's mind about the location you have chosen.

Once you have identified the location, create a list that involves as many relevant descriptive phrases as you can. You want to generate ideas of how you will describe the place to people throughout the book and creating these ideas beforehand will ensure that you are not at a loss for words or repeating your descriptions throughout the book. Having this list will help you create a dynamic description that truly helps bring the book to life for your readers and prevents them from becoming bored of the same descriptions being used over and over again.

If You Have Many Locations

If you have many locations you want to essentially conduct what you did for one location, only for many. This part of the process may seem fairly straightforward, so we are not going to further explore the process for identifying each unique location. However, there are other things you need to consider when you are using many locations in your book.

First, you want to decide which location is going to be "home" for your characters. This one, in addition to the one where your characters stay in for the longest period of time, should be the ones that you know about the most. You should have plenty of describing factors that help set the scene for what home is like for your characters, as well as for what their new place of residence is like. For example, you might set the scene for home as "The Rocky Mountains: a place where the air is cool and crisp, and the mountainous view is one that cannot be done justice short of seeing it yourself. The community is warm and cozy, especially in the cold winters when snow makes it difficult just to leave your front door." Whereas the new place of residence is described as "The prairies, where the wheat grows for miles and you can see the entire story of the sky as clouds dance across the wide-open view in front of you. The communities are cheerful and bright, and you feel like there is nowhere you can't go, and nothing to stop you from getting where you want to be." You want to describe both the location as previously mentioned and go into detail about the emotion behind each location and why these emotions differ for the protagonist.

Second, you want to identify the mode of travel if any will be used in the book. You also want to become as descriptive as possible when it comes to the mode of transport. Where does the character get on and off of it? What stands out about this mode of transport and how does it contribute to the overall story? Is there anything particular that the reader should know that will help them feel as though they are genuinely walking up to, entering, riding, and exiting the mode of transport that you have chosen? Describing the transport itself in advance will help when it comes to foreshadowing and other story-telling tactics during the writing process. Rather than leaving it up to surprise you can easily blend it into your story so that it flows effortlessly with everything you have already written up until that point, and afterward.

If You Are Making Up the Location

If you are writing a fantasy novel where you are going to be making the location up, it is important that you take the time to actually create a location that makes sense. The location you create needs to be consistent and should be relevant to the story you are telling. There are a few tips when it comes to making up a location that you can consider using to help you create an incredible location for your book.

First, consider basing your location off of somewhere that already exists. If there is somewhere on the globe that resembles what you want your fantasy world to look like, consider first creating a descriptive location setting for that place and then alternating parts of it to fulfill your fantasy world. This will assist you with keeping everything relevant and consistent across your world.

If you are going to be making up the world entirely then you want to take your time. Close your eyes and picture this world in your own mind, first. Then, write as many descriptive factors as you can about the appearance of this location. Ultimately, you want the reader to see exactly what you are seeing in your mind at the time.

You want to make sure that when you are introducing readers to your fantasy world that they feel as though they are mentally stepping into it. They should be able to find enough information in your novel that they can not only step into the world, but they can also interact with it. They should know what type of wildlife - if any - exists in the world. Give them an idea of what the colors are like, how the communities are built, what the buildings themselves look like, and what smells they can find floating around in the air. Give them an idea of what objects are around the setting so that they can mentally picture them and that they truly feel as though they are living in your imaginary world alongside your characters. This will provide you with a strong fantasy setting that will ensure that your book truly is a fantastic read.

If You Only Have One Time Period

When it comes to time periods you need to be very specific and careful. You want to choose one that would make sense to and be relevant to the story you are telling. You also want to ensure that you do enough research about it that you tell the story as though it truly is set in that time frame. A painful mistake that would truly detract from the value of your novel would be one where you choose a certain time frame and then include information that is completely irrelevant to that time frame. For example, if you chose to set your romance novel in the late 1900s but included technology such as cell phones or computers, it would not make sense to the story and would take away from the reading experience.

When you are setting the time frame you want to ensure that you do plenty of research about it. You also want to research your chosen location with relevance to the time frame. What did it look like during that time frame? What was the culture like? What were the people like? How did they treat each other? What was the common slang for that era? You want to be very specific on what it truly would have been like during that time frame so that you can walk your reader through it. Give them the opportunity to feel as though they have stepped into a time portal and they are being transported into that era, whether it be in the present or in the past.

If You Have Many Time Periods

When you are writing a story that has many time periods the tactics you use to develop the setting is similar to if you are writing a story that has many locations. Essentially, you want to ensure that you are effectively researching each time period so that you can provide relevant and factual information based on each time period. You really need to stay focused on the details you are providing so that your reader can easily be walked back and forth with you without finding irrelevant or false pieces of information anywhere within' the text. The more focused and factual you are, the better. When it comes to developing many time periods in a story, there is not much more required than you repeating the research processes several times over for each time period you will write about. Something you may want to add, however, is the mode of transportation being used to transport across time periods. Be sure that you create a piece of machinery and provide enough details about it that you can explain how it works and create a graphic image of it in the minds of your readers.

If You Are Making up the Time Period

If you are making up a time period in your novel, then you need to be extremely descriptive about this time period. You should identify what the time period is, and why it does not already exist. For example, maybe you are generating your own fantasy setting on an alternate planet and Earth has yet to exist therefore the time is not yet in history. Or, perhaps you are writing one in the future and the time has not happened yet, so you are creating it yourself. You need to be able to thoroughly understand *why* you are creating this new time period so that your readers understand as well.

In addition to knowing why, you also need to make up all of the important details about the time period. What is the culture like in this time period? What form of government or authority exists? What do people speak like? Are there any slang words used that your readers may not already know? What do these slang words mean? How do people treat each other? What parts of the community are different from anything we experience in our own world? What else sets this time period apart from what you are presently living or what we already know about? You want to make sure that you go into detail beforehand about creating this time period so that when it comes to the writing process you already know. Doing this will ensure that you stay consistent with your novel and that nothing is added that is then forgotten about and later contradicted. When you are making something up entirely it is important that you put the effort in towards making it truly believable for your readers. This will ensure that they are able to follow the story and that it flows well without having any contradictions, confusing pieces of information, or other additions that otherwise take away from the quality of the story itself.

Combining the Two

The setting of your story is a combination of the time period and the location. When you have completely researched or created each the location and the time period, you must then combine the two. This part of the process is simple, but it is important. You want to make sure that you identify anywhere in the combination where information might contradict itself or take away from the reading experience. For example, if you are writing a book set in the present about an Amish colony that still operates without running water or electricity, you need to identify these factors and explain the discrepancy. Making sure that your time and location mesh together seamlessly and that anything contradictory is explained will ensure that you have a strong setting for your story. This means that you will be able to easily and effortlessly guide your readers through the book without any part of it leading to them wondering what is truly going on with your story.

Questions to Ask Yourself

The following questions are questions you should ask yourself when you are developing your setting. This will ensure that you have a strong plan for your setting and that no details are missed out on.

1. What location(s) will my story take place in?

2. What is unique to this location?

3. How could I describe this location in five sentences or less?

4. When I read that description, can I truly see the location in my mind?

5. Are there any further descriptions I could use to strengthen the visual of my location?

6. What time period(s) will my story take place in?

7. What is unique to this time period?

8. How could I describe this location in five sentences or less?

9. When I read that description, can I truly feel and sense the time period in my mind?

10. Are there any further descriptions I could add to enrich the time period in my story?

11. Do my time period and location make sense together?

12. What describing factors can I use to explain any
discrepancies between my location and time period,
if there are any?

Chapter 3: The Point of View

The next part of writing your story requires you to consider which point of view you want to write from. As an author, you have the opportunity to decide exactly how the reader is going to learn about different elements of your story, as well as how those elements will feel to them. You can do this directly through the use of point of view and which you choose to write your story in.

There are a few different points of view that you can write from when it comes to storytelling. Each one has a unique element that allows you to elaborate on and recall experiences within' the story in a certain way. Some will limit you to only telling it from one perspective whereas others allow you to elaborate with multiple perspectives, or even to provide "outsiders" insight into different experiences. How you choose your point of view will also depend on a few things. Before you choose one, however, let's explore each unique point of view and the advantages and disadvantages it provides you with as a storyteller.

First Person

First person point of view is one of the most popular choices when it comes to writing novels. This is the point of view where the writer refers to the narrator as "I", "we", "me", "mine", "my", and "us". This is similar to if you were telling a story from your own past to someone who was standing in front of you. When you are telling a story from the first-person point of view you must pick which protagonist is going to be the storyteller in your book. Typically, it is the heroic character or the one that is involved in the majority of the scenes that will be chosen as the first-person narrator. However, you can choose virtually anyone you want, dependent upon who is going to be the best angle for you to speak from.

When you write in the first person, you provide a very natural flow to your story. Your reader will feel as though you are telling them *your* story, and if you can effectively captivate them then it will actually begin to feel like your reader is the narrator. Using "I" sentiments and first-person narrative allows your reader to fully immerse themselves in the novel and get a true, deep insight into how the narrator was feeling during each scene. You also only have to pay attention to and fully develop the mind of one character: the narrators. This is the one that you will need to have the most insight to. The rest will be based on how the narrator perceives them, which means that you don't have to go quite as deep or know every minute detail of each person. However, this can also lead to some disadvantages. For example, you are limited to only reflecting on and elaborating the story based on what the narrator would feel. You cannot explore anyone else's feelings unless you use tactics such as conversation to help the narrative character explore the feelings and thoughts of another. While this is an effective tactic, you aren't going to be able to use it in every single scene or the story will sound strange and unnatural. Furthermore, the narrative character must always be involved in or at the center of every event that takes place in the book. Otherwise, large portions are going to be missed or you are going to bounce between different points of view which is not effective.

Some ways that people have managed to use the first-person narrative while still maintaining the insights on several characters at once is by developing books whereby each chapter or section is narrated by a different character. This provides the reader with the opportunity to see into several different characters and their experiences, but it can also jolt the flow of your story and result in your readers struggling to really connect with each character the way they could if you maintained a single first-person narrative.

Second Person

Second person is an undesirable choice when it comes to writing fiction, but some people choose to use it when they are writing short stories. This is an interesting point of view to write from, but it rarely creates the ability for an author to produce an entire novel without the novel sounding strange and lacking natural flow. Second person is the "you" narrative, whereby you refer to the person reading or the narrator as "you". For example, "you were standing on a street corner when suddenly someone bumped into you." The entire book would be written in this point of view which, as you might be able to tell, is not ideal. While some books have been written this way, most publishers advise against it and will even refuse to publish books that have been written in this narrative.

The only advantage to writing in the second person narrative is that your book will be unique and eccentric. Based on the nature of this narrative you gain the ability to speak directly to the reader which can be an interesting technique, but it also does not offer you a strong advantage in storytelling. For the most part, anything written in the second person narrative that is longer than a few hundred words feels uncomfortable and sounds "off" to the reader. They will likely grow tired of the eccentric feel and simply begin feeling as though the writing is uncomfortable and strange. Furthermore, it says that you are unprofessional and are inexperienced when it comes to novels. Unless you are a highly experienced writer who has already developed a name for themselves, it is typically best that you avoid this point of view.

Third Person

Third person is the point of view whereby someone completely outside of the story is telling it. For example, using identifiers such as "he" or "she" instead of "I" or "you". This point of view is another popular one when it comes to writing fiction novels because it provides the author with the ability to provide insight into many different elements of each character. It also provides the author with a greater ability to influence the reader's emotions towards various characters without that influence being limited to what would be true and natural for any given character within' the book. For example, perhaps the protagonist hates the antagonist for something he's done wrong. In the first person, you would be required to establish feelings of hatred towards the antagonist. In the third person, however, you can further explain the situation and provide the reader with insight as to how it was a mistake and the protagonist was carrying a grudge over something that was a misunderstanding, for example. It provides you with a stronger power to shape and influence the story in a highly unique way.

When it comes to writing in the third party there are two different types you can write in: third person limited omniscience, or third person unlimited omniscience. Since each one is so unique, we are going to explore them in two different subsections below.

Before we dive in, however, please note that in the following subsections we will discuss a tool many authors use whereby they speak in the third person from a different character's point of view in each scene or chapter. This helps naturally break up the story without confusing the reader along the way. This should not be confused with the technique whereby authors write one chapter per character from the first-person point of view. Although the techniques are virtually the same, they do involve writing from a different point of view in each style.

Third Person Limited Omniscience

Third person limited omniscience means that the author has the power to enter the mind of only a few characters within' the novel. Usually, during this type of experience, the author would write from the point of view of one character per chapter or per scene to avoid confusion. When it comes to this viewpoint, the author would still write with the "he" or "she" descriptors, but would primarily focus on one character per scene or chapter.

This point of view provides the author with the opportunity to enrich the experience by providing viewpoints from many different characters, thereby giving the reader a greater amount of detail and depth into each scene and experience within' the book. It also provides the author the opportunity to write from a broader scope where they are not required to limit their story to a single person's experiences. Instead, you can elaborate on experiences that may take place without one or more of the character's present. The biggest disadvantage of this is that for the author it requires you to take more time to make each part of the book flow naturally, as well as to provide distinctive voices for each character so as not to confuse yourself or your reader. Furthermore, if you switch too often you will break up the flow of your story and create an unnatural and uncomfortable. It is important that you take your time and truly dedicate if you are going to use this practice, also. Many authors find that they write in this point of view for a few chapters and then they wind up writing from the first-person narrative for the remainder of the book. This laziness can result in your first chapters, or last chapters needing to be repaired so that the entire book is written in the same narrative and flows smoothly.

Third Person Unlimited Omniscience

Third person, unlimited omniscience is virtually the same as limited omniscience, except that the author is not restricted to only sharing the experience from a few character's points of view. Instead, they can shift into the mind of any character within' the story and provide their viewpoint on the events that are taking place.

While this may provide the author with the opportunity to elaborate and provide great detail and depth to the story, it can also result in them getting far too carried away if they are not careful. Writing from too many different points of view can diffuse the entire story and result in the author washing out any storyline that may have taken place. It is similar to the mistake of oversharing or otherwise providing far too much information, well beyond what the reader needs to know. Although it may give them a strong understanding of each scene, it can also cause for it to take far too long to "get to the point already". It is generally advised against the idea of you writing in third person unlimited omniscience unless you are using the technique strategically to avoid damaging your storyline.

How to Choose

There is one incredibly each tactic to use when it comes to deciding which point of view you want to use when it comes to sharing your story. Consider taking one small scene from the book and then writing that scene in three different narratives: first person, third person limited omniscience, and third person unlimited omniscience. Only write a few short paragraphs in each point of view so that it doesn't take too long, but be sure that you write them well. Then, read each one. This will give you an idea as to how each point of view would shape the reader's experience and what "feel" it gives to your story. It also provides you with some practice as to how each point of view feels as the author and if it gives you the ability to express yourself in the way that you want to be expressed.

Questions to Ask Yourself

The following questions are questions you should ask yourself when you are choosing your point of view. This will ensure that you have a strong plan for your point of view and that no details are missed out on.

1. Who do I want to tell my story?

2. What feeling do I want my readers to have?

3. Which point of view is going to be reasonable for me to write an entire novel in?

4. Will this give me the opportunity to express my
    story the way I want to?

5. Is there any way that this might limit my story or
    otherwise hinder the reader's experience?

Chapter 4: Characters

Naturally, your story needs characters. After all, what story are you telling if there is no one taking part in the story itself? Creating a strong story requires for you to have strong, well-developed characters involved. If you are looking for greater insight as to how you can develop well-rounded characters I encourage you to read book 6 from this series: *"Character Development*: Step-by-Step."* Because I provide you with such great detail on how to develop your characters in that novel, I will not go into elaborate detail on character development in this chapter. Instead, we are going to identify other important information about your characters, such as who needs to be involved in the story and how they contribute. Knowing this basic information is powerful in regard to the actual writing process. This will help you when it comes to outlining and creating a plan for the direction of your story. When it comes to the actual writing process, however, you will want to make sure that you have fully developed characters so that they are realistic and can add to your story in a powerful way. In the meantime, let's explore other important aspects of characters in your story.

The Value of Your Characters

Characters are a powerful element of your story because they truly drive the story forward. Without characters, the story simply cannot move forward because there would be nothing to talk about. Your characters help you not only convey the story but also express it in certain ways. Depending on what point of view you have chosen, your characters can be used in unique ways to manipulate the reader's thoughts and feelings about other characters, as well as about the storyline and events that take place within' the story.

Think of professional dancers. Music is put on as the foundation for the story and it can be related to the setting. The words that coincide with the music, or the song lyrics, are responsible for providing you with insight into what the song is about. Once the dancers begin dancing, however, they can manipulate how you feel about the song, what emotions are provoked within' you, and how you take in the experience as a whole. Without the dancers, it would simply be a song with lyrics. With the dancers, it is a story with a soul.

The same goes with writing books. The setting is the foundation for your story, and the narrator is the one who tells the story. Your characters, however, provide the heart and soul of your story. They are the ones that you can use to help manipulate the readers' thoughts and provoke different emotions in them so that they experience the book in the way that you want them to. While each unique reader may have a slightly different experience, the overall interpretation of the book will remain fairly similar if you use your tools or characters, properly.

Choosing Your Protagonist

Because of how important characters are, it is vital that you choose a good character to be your protagonist. Your protagonist needs to be a strong character who can lead the story in a powerful way. When you are putting together the outline and idea for your story, consider which specific character would be best at bringing readers through the story in an effective manner that would allow you to create the experience you want to create. Which of your characters will be involved in the most experiences? Which ones will have the best emotional attachment to the storyline so that they can move your readers for you? If you are writing from a first-person narrative, you need to choose a single character that is going to be able to effectively move everyone through the entire novel. For example, it may be the wife, best friend, teacher, and book club host. Because this particular character is involved in so many different elements of the community she may be the best individual and voice to help you tell the story with a great level of depth and dynamic so that the reader truly has an incredible experience. If you are writing in the third party, however, make sure that you choose powerful characters that you will write from. These would-be ones that all connect in one way or another and that have stories that will link together. This ensures that each character makes sense to the narrative. If you are writing in third-party unlimited omniscience, make sure that when you move to the narrative of someone who may be new or unique to a specific part of the story that this move makes sense and it is clear to the reader as to why you are doing this. This will ensure that you are drawing the reader through a clear and logical storyline that makes sense.

How Many Characters Do You Really Need?

The number of characters you choose to have in your story is really unique to the story you are trying to tell. If you are telling a romance novel, for example, you may only have two primary characters and a handful of other characters that contribute to the story. For example, some best friends, family members, the cashier at the drug store they always stop at, or the receptionist at the hotel where they celebrate their honeymoon. When you are planning your story, you need to consider how many characters are actually going to be required in order for you to tell the story. As you carry on you may discover that you need to add more characters along the way, so it is not mandatory for you to identify every single character you are going to write about immediately. However, you should have a good idea of who your primary and secondary characters are going to be. Remember, your primary characters are the ones that show up in nearly all scenes and your secondary ones are characters that are recurring in a major way.

What Your Characters Say About Your Book

The characters you choose are going to say a lot about the book you are writing and the story you are telling. These characters have the power to shape the reader's perception of the book, as well as gain an even deeper insight as to what the setting is like and the feelings they should be deriving from the general information you are providing. For example, if you are writing a book from the late 1990's about a town in the southern states, you could write about a wealthy family or a poor family. This would shape your character's point of view on the entire setting and emotions associated with the book, as well as how they perceive your characters. It also helps round out your story. The characters you choose, how you design them, and how you portray them will all contribute to the story you tell. In the previous example, one story might provide the reader with a country glamorous feeling where they ride horses and own a large farm with stable hands, whereas the other might provide your family with a poorer country feel where they *are* the stable hands and they live in a shack built on the corner of the property. Who you choose for your characters will provide greater depth for your story and ultimately be the final factor that provides your reader with the clear picture of what they see, think, and feel as they read the story you have written for them.

Questions to Ask Yourself

The following questions are questions you should ask yourself when you are developing the basic outline for your characters. This will ensure that you have a strong plan for your character development and that no details are missed out on. Remember to check out book 6 where we go deeper into the creation and development of characters so that you have a strong selection of characters to help move your story forward.

1. What story am I telling and who is the focus of the story?

2. What point of view am I writing in and whose point of view do I want to write from?

3. What recurring characters are an important element of this story?

4. Are there any additional characters that will be involved in key plot points?

5. How do these specific characters help move the story?

Chapter 5: Conflict

Every good novel comes with a fair amount of conflict involved. If there was no conflict, then there would be nothing that really keeps the reader engaged. Everyone loves a great happy-ending story, but most like to see the work that goes into creating that happy ending. This is somewhat like providing a realistic snippet of your character's lives to your readers. No one's real life is easy all of the time, so writing an entire novel where all of your characters never experience any true conflict is not only unrealistic but also boring. It takes away from the entire reading experience by never giving any depth or diversity to your story.

Creating conflict in your novel should be an ongoing process. It is not simply about having one major conflict and everything being sunshine and rainbows up until and after that point. Instead, it is about leading up to the conflict, and about coming down from it as well. You want to have one primary conflict that drives the story, but you should include many other conflicts along the way as well. These smaller conflicts add more depth and reality to your story, but they also help you lead your reader through many triumphs and victories with the characters. Each time your character overcomes something your reader will feel as though they overcame it together and it will bond the reader to your character even more. Furthermore, it stops you from writing an unrealistic story that goes from bad to much worse and then suddenly great again. It provides you with a natural and lifelike flow that allows your reader to feel as though they are genuinely connecting with an individual and not a character that you have made up for the purpose of writing a novel.

Types of Conflict

There are a couple of different types of conflict that exist in every novel. The first one is considered a primary conflict. This is the primary purpose of why you are telling the story, and it is what you will lead up to and wind down from throughout the process of writing the novel. This is the "big one" that will keep your readers engaged and have them feeling like they *need* to know what happens after that particular conflict takes place.

The next type is secondary conflict. This is the type of conflict that takes place leading up to and after the primary conflict. These are smaller conflicts that exist in addition to the primary conflict. For example, maybe in an action-based novel the kidnapper is about to drive a car off of a bridge, so the protagonist has to go save the person who has been kidnapped, but they can't do that until they can get a car because the kidnapper has their car. Here, the kidnapper driving off the bridge would be the primary conflict and the lack of a car would be the secondary conflict. In the grand scheme of the entire story, however, both would be secondary to the greater problem which is that someone has been kidnapped. When you build on the conflict in this way it diversifies everything and adds a more realistic and compelling story base that drives readers forward. Now, they want to know where the protagonist gets the car from if they reach the kidnapper on time, and how they save the person who has been kidnapped. As you can see, it would keep them engaged.

The third type of conflict is an alternate conflict. In a story where third person point of view is used, the author may choose to have two or three primary conflicts going on. For example, for the parents getting divorced might be the primary conflict, for one kid her social life falling apart might be the primary conflict, and for the second kid choosing which parent to live with might be the primary conflict. This story would run with each of these conflicts equally as important as the other, and each one drives part of the story forward until it all reaches an ending whereby everyone is satisfied and happy with the outcome.

When the Conflict Should Occur

Choosing when the conflict should occur in your book is important. There are many different points at which you might desire to put the primary conflict into your plotline. However, it is imperative that you give your reader a reason to care by infusing some form of conflict into the first ten pages.

Some authors choose to start out within' the first ten pages by introducing the primary conflict and then providing the remainder of the wind-down story from there. For example, elaborating further on the plotline where someone is kidnapped, you may write that said person was kidnapped on the first page, or within' the first ten pages. The rest of the book would then be a series of secondary conflicts that result from the primary conflict, until the end where the person is rescued.

Other authors do not want to reveal the primary conflict right away and choose to save it for later. Some prefer to put it somewhere in the middle of the book and provide a fairly even amount of writing leading up to the conflict and winding down from it, whereas others like to put it towards the end of the story and use the winding down process as the opportunity to introduce the "happily ever after" experience.

Where you prefer to put the conflict in your own story heavily depends on how quickly you want your readers to move through the conflict, as well as how you want the conflict to leverage the story overall. If you want it to be the primary focus of the story, you may want to introduce it sooner or at least use secondary conflicts to suggest it starting right away. However, if you want the happily-ever-after story to be the primary focus of the story then you may want to use more casual secondary conflicts to keep the reader engaged while building them up to the conflict and then using the resolution as your final happily-ever-after scene.

Regardless of how you choose to infuse the story with your conflict, one thing remains consistent: you need to give the reader a reason to continue reading your book. Within' the first ten pages your reader needs to understand why they should fall in love with the book through developing relationships with the characters, understanding the importance of the conflicts and how they affect the characters, and what they can expect to feel when reading the book. All of this can be done by how you introduce the conflict, and when.

Questions to Ask Yourself

The following questions are questions you should ask yourself when you are developing your conflict. These questions will ensure that you are clear on what your conflict is and how it affects the story you are telling.

1. What is the primary conflict taking place in my novel?

2. How many primary conflicts do I want involved in my novel? (Note: if you are telling a story from the first person, choose one or two at most.)

3. What type of secondary conflicts can I use to build up to the primary conflict?

4. What secondary conflicts would work well to help
    me wind down from the conflict?

5. How do I want the conflict to drive my novel
    forward?

6. When do I want to introduce the conflict and how
    will that affect the reading experience?

7. Does the conflict make sense to the novel?

8. Does the conflict provide enough reason for the
    reader to truly care?

9. If I am not introducing my primary conflict right
    away, what conflict can I use to compel my reader to
    continue reading?

Chapter 6: Additional Tips

In addition to the basics of writing your novel, there are many additional tips that you can use when it comes to generating a high-quality fiction-based novel that will not only impress yourself but your audience as well. Using these tips when you are writing your story will help you increase the joy you get from the process while also increasing the value of your work. These tips are selected from a series of professional writers and have helped them in the process of generating their own fiction novels. Remember, however, not everyone is the same and therefore you may not require all of these tips when it comes to writing your own novel. Take what feels right for you and your unique story and leave the rest!

As mentioned in the introduction of this book, the tips and information provided within' this book is unique and issued to help you not only create higher quality materials but also enjoy the process. Writing your novel should be an experience that you gain joy from, not one that stresses you out or makes you feel incompetent. If you are struggling, you are not doing it right. The following tips can help take you out of the struggling mode and put you back in the mood to enjoy the experience. When the process is light and enjoyable you will likely find that you produce much better work, so be sure to slow down and readdress your approach if you are struggling to produce the results you desire.

Finally, because of the fact that some of these tips may not apply to the unique book you are writing, you will likely want to keep this information handy for any additional projects you may desire to accomplish. Some of these tips may be more relevant to certain types of books than they are to others, therefore you are likely to find value in new and unique ways each time you return to this book.

Think Outside of the Box

When it comes to writing stories, there are many plotlines that exist that are simply rewritten with different angles and different characters. The setting may be different and some of the events that take place may alter, but ultimately the entire story works out to be similar to several other books within' the same genre. Although the saying "don't try to reinvent the wheel" may ring true in many cases, it is not always the best approach to take when you are attempting to write a new and interesting book that will engage your readers in a powerful way.

Instead of trying to recreate a tired plotline, try thinking outside of the box entirely. Consider the genre you are writing for, such as romance, mystery, or fantasy, and spend some time thinking about parts of the story that are never typically told within' traditional novels from that genre. As you discover new parts of the story that you can emphasize on, make sure that you are truly criticizing them to ensure that there is a good reason as to why this part of the story hasn't been told before. Sometimes a certain element may be rejected or ignored because there simply isn't enough to talk about, other times it may be because that isn't the traditional approach, therefore, most people don't consider it when they are writing a novel in that genre.

Looking at things from a different perspective and discovering new ways to share a story provides your book with a unique twist that allows you to engage your readers not only through incredible work but also through the element of surprise. For example, most romance novels lead up to the part where the lovers fall in love, but what if your novel was more focused on the wind-down? What if the marriage happened within' the first ten pages and from there it was the wind-down and told the next part of the romance story that most novels don't focus on? Paying attention to unique elements of the story gives you the opportunity to still write in your chosen genre while also having the chance to put a unique spin on things and create a story that people weren't expecting.

Ditch Expectations

When it comes to the writing world you will likely stumble on expectations from many different people. Publishers, readers, yourself, other authors, everyone has an expectation of what a book "should" be like. While it is important to consider these elements, especially since some of them can make or break the success of your book, it is also important to ditch the pressure that comes along with them.

Most writers can agree that feeling too much pressure can result in writer's block and it can also drown the enjoyment you gain from writing the book. It can make it feel too much like work and less like an experience to be enjoyed by both you and the readers. Instead of putting that much pressure on yourself, ditch expectations and write for the trashcan. You will likely be surprised at the quality of work you produce when you aren't considering all of the technical aspects of your book.

Set Deadlines

Having deadlines set in place can help you keep motivated, and it can also help you plan for other parts of the book writing process. For example, this can help you decide when you need to begin approaching publishers when work needs to be handed in, when marketing efforts should commence, and more. Having deadlines in place keeps everything moving forward and prevents you from avoiding or neglecting your book altogether.

When you are setting deadlines, however, be generous with yourself. Do not set a deadline that is fixed on a date that requires you to work an obscene amount each day from where you are now until the deadline arrives. Doing this will bring back the pressure and take away the joy of the writing experience. Instead of writing and allowing the story to flow through you, you will be writing under the pressure of knowing that if you don't get a certain amount of words out *right now* that you will officially be late for your deadline and everything will be hindered by your lack of writing speed. Instead, choose a generous deadline that gives you plenty of time to take breaks, step aside and get a breather, and come back to your work to finish it. Be kind to yourself and account for breaks. Most writers do not write an entire book in one straight shot. Instead, they write for several days, or even weeks, and then take breaks off in between to allow for more inspiration to come to them before they carry on. Give yourself the opportunity to have these breaks so that you can take them without feeling pressure.

Get a Good "Test" Reader

When your book is complete, you need to have a good test reader who can read through it for you. This is someone who is not necessarily looking for grammatical errors or otherwise editing your book. Rather, they are simply reading to see if it is engaging and if it will actually appeal to your audience. Naturally, this person should identify with your target audience or their opinion may not count for much.

It is important that you do not hand your book to everyone you know and get as many people as possible. Instead, pick one or *maybe* two test readers who identify with your target audience and allow them to read the book. This way you can get honest opinions without feeling overwhelmed by a number of responses you get. It also helps open your purchasing audience because your friends and family will likely be some of your earliest buyers once your title is launched.

Avoid Perfectionism

Many writers put a pressure on themselves to create the perfect piece of work. They may think of an artist they already know or a series of books they have read that they perceive as perfect and they want their books to be the same quality. Understand that this is not valuable to the writing process and it can actually hold you back from producing high-quality work.

Perfectionism can be intimidating, and it can have you overly critical of the work you are producing. Most of the best books that exist on shelves today were not subjected to perfectionism. Instead, the author focused on telling a great story, not a perfect one. Readers are not expecting a perfect book, they are expecting one that takes them through the story in such a way that is engaging and makes them genuinely feel as though they are present and can relate to what they are reading. Perfectionists need not worry.

Write What You Don't Know

There is a long-standing piece of advice that tells writers to "write what they know", but this isn't always the best way to go. Unless you are deeply passionate about your topic and can infuse it with all of the emotions related to that passion, consider writing what you *don't* know.

Think about a topic that interests you and things you would have to learn based on that new interest. Then, spend time researching it for the purpose of writing the book. For example, if your protagonist is a karate star, consider going to a few karate lessons to get a first-hand idea of what it is like so that you can write from within' the experience. Writing in this way gives you a better opportunity to convey the excitement that you are feeling through your story, thus translating it into the reader's experience.

When we write about what we know, we often don't have the same level of excitement or passion as we would if we were brand new to the knowledge because we have a "been there, done that" feeling towards the topic. Even when we are passionate about it, it can be hard to convey that new childlike wonder through the story. When you are brand new, however, it is brand new to you *and* the reader, and it can enhance the quality of your story through all of the exciting emotions you infuse it with.

Manipulate Your Reader's Emotions

Readers are most often attracted to books that draw out a variety of emotions in them. You want to use your characters and the storyline to manipulate your reader's emotions so that they are emotionally drawn to and attached to the book as you are reading. Many readers agree that the best books are the ones that leave you with a "lost" feeling when you put them down. This is because the reader has developed an emotional attachment to the book, likely based on the writer's technique.

You can manipulate your reader's emotions through a variety of different plot points, experiences, and descriptive phrases. You want to start by helping them become emotionally connected to one or more of the characters, then subject these characters to various experiences that draw out certain emotions in the characters. As a result, it will draw out emotions in your readers as well.

When your reader is emotionally connected to the book, they are far more engaged and much more likely to read it all the way through. Furthermore, they are much more likely to genuinely enjoy the book. Make sure that you play with several different emotions so that the book is not excessively sad, angry, funny, or otherwise. Even if you want to emphasize on one emotion more than the rest, be sure to add a healthy mixture of other emotions so that the book does not become predictable or boring.

Conclusion

Thank you for reading *"How to Write a Novel: Step by Step | Essential Romance Novel, Mystery Novel and Fantasy Novel Writing Tricks Any Writer Can Learn"*!

I hope that this book was able to provide you with many tips and tricks to assist you in the process of writing your very own fiction novel. Whether you are writing a romance novel, a mystery novel, or a fantasy novel, I hope that you were able to learn many valuable methods to increase the enjoyment of the experience and increase the quality of your work overall. This book was designed to help you master the writing process, and I hope that you were able to learn plenty of new and diverse information in order to help you do so.

The next step is to start writing! If you haven't already, begin with your outline and move forward from there. As you are working on your book, be sure to check back with this guidebook regularly to see if there are any tips or tricks related to the part of the process you are presently in. This book was written to be a writing resource that you can check back to as often as you need, so don't hesitate to keep it handy during the entire writing process. You never know what part of the book might become valuable to you during each unique part of the process!

Thank you, and enjoy!